Faith and Politics
in the Life of Moses

MARKETPLACE INSTITUTE

The Regent College Marketplace Institute is a theological research and design institute at Regent College in Vancouver, Canada, committed to the communication of the gospel as public truth. The Institute develops resources, frameworks, and tools for integrating faith and public life, in order to support the transformation of individuals, communities, sectors, and the marketplace of ideas.

Faith and Politics in the Life of Moses

Preston Manning

Regent College Publishing
www.regentpublishing.com

Faith and Politics in the Life of Moses
Copyright © 2013 Preston Manning

All rights reserved. No part of this publication may be reproduced, stored in a retrieval system, or transmitted, in any form or by any means, electronic, mechanical, photocopying, recording or otherwise, without the prior written permission of the author, except in the case of brief quotations embodied in critical articles and reviews.

Published 2013 by Regent College Publishing
for the Regent College Marketplace Institute
http://marketplace.regent-college.edu

Regent College Publishing
5800 University Boulevard, Vancouver, BC V6T 2E4 Canada
Web: www.regentpublishing.com
E-mail: info@regentpublishing.com

Regent College Publishing is an imprint of the Regent Bookstore <www.regentbookstore.com>. Views expressed in works published by Regent College Publishing are those of the author and do not necessarily represent the official position of Regent College <www.regent-college.edu>.

ISBN 978-1-57383-494-0

Cataloguing in Publication information is on file at Library and Archives Canada.

Contents

Introduction   7

1. The Call to Involvement   11
2. At Work with God   23
3. The Rule of Law   35
4. The Role of the Leader   47
5. The Challenges of Leadership   57
6. Last Words   69

Introduction

The mission of the Marketplace Institute at Regent College is to help Christians connect the gospel of Christ with every aspect of life: culture, science, media, business, and, yes, politics.

As citizens of the Kingdom of God but also citizens of our country and the world, we are affected by domestic and international politics in a myriad of ways. Politics affects our freedoms and responsibilities, who governs us and how, the type of education our children receive, our incomes and employment opportunities, our taxes and what they are used for, the quality of our environment, our health and old age security, our collective response to the needs of the poor and oppressed, the safety of our streets, and whether we live in a time of war or a time of peace.

At the Marketplace Institute, we believe that Jesus' call is for his followers to be salt and light, to be ambassadors for Him, to carry out the ministry of reconciliation, and to communicate the truth of the gospel to every nation. This is a call to relate the truth and person of Christ to every sphere of life, including the political.

One way of doing so is to study the lives and experience of God's servants in the past who have been called to involvement in the politics of their day. Such studies are particularly relevant when they are conducted through the eyes and interpreted through the experiences of contemporary Christians who have been involved in the politics of our day.

Hence, this study, which is titled *Faith and Politics in the Life of Moses* and authored by Preston Manning, a practicing Christian, Senior Fellow of the Marketplace Institute, founder of two Canadian federal political parties, and former Leader of the Official Opposition in the Canadian House of Commons.

From a secular standpoint, Moses—one of the best-known religious and political leaders in history—encountered virtually every trial and circumstance that a modern political leader faces: fierce opposition from external opponents; the burden of overwork and the need to delegate; the challenges of executive decision making, administration, and law making; threats to his leadership from his closest associates (arguably the most trying form of opposition a political leader faces); continuous criticism and complaining from his followers; shortages of resources; the charge that he had broken his promises; outright rebellion against his leadership; the roller coaster ride between great accomplishments and profound disappointments; the strains that political leadership puts on family life; and the problem of succession.

At the same time, Moses was a political leader whose intimate relationship with Jehovah involved the following: providential positioning; a sense of divine calling; numerous experiences with the miraculous; a constant effort to discern Jehovah's will with respect to governance; the communication and enforcement of God-inspired laws and standards; lawmaking, particularly in relation to morality, mediation, and intercession; encounters with evil in all its forms; the challenge of maintaining the spirit of the laws in competition with their material and ceremonial embodiments; and the reception and interpretation of revelations of the character of God which profoundly affected his political and spiritual leadership.

There is, therefore, much for contemporary Christians with political interests and ambitions to learn from the life of Moses, especially as interpreted by a contemporary Christian with significant political experience.

In the following pages, please join us as we study "Faith and Politics in the Life of Moses."

1

The Call to Involvement

Democratic societies, such as Canada, require the critical engagement of its members—to vote, to run for political office, and to engage in all forms of advocacy in between. So how does one discern the call to engage in advocacy in the form of pursuing political office? This first chapter in this study explores the answer to this very question, and addresses many implications of the discernment process. Does God actually call believers to political involvement? Or might we be deceived by ulterior ambitions? Scripture sheds considerable light on questions such as these, particularly through the life of Moses.

Providential Positioning

Calling begins long before any burning bush. We can first recognize the particular calling placed on Moses in his providential positioning—in his unique position in infancy, personal and cultural heritage, and external circumstances. Moses would eventually be called of God to perform specific political and spiritual tasks, liberating the Israelites from bondage in Egypt and communicating the laws of God to them. But he was first born into a Hebrew family, miraculously rescued from the waters of the Nile by an Egyptian princess, and raised by his own mother in Pharaoh's household (Exodus 2:1–12). What, then, does one's positioning by birth, personal and cultural heritage, and circumstances suggest in terms of possible future political and spiritual activity?

In my case, I was raised in both an evangelical Christian home and a political home; my father was elected to the Alberta Legislature in the midst of the Great Depression and served there for thirty-three years, twenty-five as Premier. Although my father never encouraged me to become directly active in the political sphere, I absorbed enough of politics, government, and western Canadian political history to have a sense of the most appropriate time to enter politics—especially if one wanted to create a new political movement in the western Canadian tradition.

We must, of course, exercise caution—which demands spiritual discernment—in interpreting any providential leading from one's positioning by birth, personal and cultural heritage, or circumstances. For every Moses, you can point to another instance in which there was little by way of this kind of positioning. For instance, there is little to suggest that the shepherd boy David was being prepared to be King of Israel (other than that herding sheep is good preparation for politics, as some cynics have suggested). Yet David became one of God's greatest political and spiritual leaders. We need wisdom to interpret where our positioning might—or might not—be providentially leading us.

Moses' Future Mission

Having found himself in a providential position, there is much Moses still did not know about his calling or future mission. What Moses does see from where he stands is the injustice being done to his own people by the Egyptians and amongst the Israelites themselves. In response to this, something—one might argue divine prompting—impels him to do something, to take action, to intervene. However, his intervention fails, and this failure of his first attempt to exert political leadership shakes to the core his self-confidence as a potential liberator and leader of Israel. As a result, Moses is forced to flee Egypt and begins a forty-year exile in Midian herding sheep on the backside of the desert (Exodus 2:11–23).

For someone who seems to be providentially positioned to intervene where there truly is injustice, Moses' situation raises some questions. First of all, should Moses have waited on God for more specific leading and instruction on the how (God's way) and the when (God's timing) of the liberation of Israel?[1] Secondly, was this a necessary step in Moses' journey as a leader? It might be argued that Moses' confidence in himself as a potential liberator and leader of Israel needed to be shaken to the core before God could use him in such capacities.

Applying these considerations to our own situations, we can ask, How inclined are we to wait on God until we have clear direction, and how do we reconcile this need to wait with the apparent need to seize an opportunity? Secondly, where, what, or who is the source of that confidence in our ability to contribute or lead politically? These are questions with which I have wrestled, and that wrestling has led me to the realization that in politics "timing is everything." There is a time to take advantage of the situation and a time to wait patiently. As Brutus more eloquently put it in Shakespeare's *Julius Caesar*:

> There is a tide in the affairs of men,
> Which, taken at the flood, leads on to fortune;
> Omitted all the voyage of their life
> Is bound in shallows and in miseries.
> On such a full sea are we now afloat,

> And we must take the current when it serves,
> Or lose our ventures.
> —Act 4, scene 3

My own approach to discerning correct timing was that when I saw a long-run political opportunity on the distant horizon I would question whether this "revelation" was God-given or not. Then, unless otherwise directed, I would pray for God's guidance and blessing on the seizure of the opportunity.

Moses' Direct Calling

In addition to the positional calling Moses received, he also received what might be called a direct calling—the story of the burning bush. In fact, God's communication with Moses at the burning bush (Exodus 4) is perhaps the seminal experience of God's direct calling in Moses' life.

Importantly, God begins by giving Moses a special revelation of himself. It is at the burning bush that God reveals himself to Moses as the eternally present one—the "I Am" (Exodus 3:13–15). This is the first of four special revelations of the nature and character of God received by Moses during his lifetime, which we will continue to explore throughout this series.

One might conclude, therefore, that a fresh revelation of the nature and character of God is a key dimension of any direct calling. In Moses' case—as in the commissioning of Isaiah (Isaiah 6)—the I Am of God precedes the call to go and do. The revelation precedes the receiving of the particular assignment. (This is a concept that will be explored further in the next article of the series.)

Having revealed himself in a spectacular way, God then informs Moses what he is doing, and what he intends to do with respect to the liberation of Israel (Exodus 7:3–10). Having heard what God is doing, Moses' assignment is to join in—to partner, as it were—with God in the liberating work. This way of working is quite different from Moses' first undertaking to liberate Israel independent of God's help. In particular, God tells Moses that he has come down to liberate his people and will bring them to the Promised Land. Moses is instructed to return to Egypt so that he can join in this work and help bring it about.

We can thus see God's revelation of what he himself is doing as a second dimension of Moses' direct calling because it allows Moses to join in that work. This same theme was emphasized by Jesus himself when he explained his own calling to "the very work that the Father has given me to finish" (John 5:36). As he says earlier, "My Father is always at work to this very day, and I, too, am working." Furthermore, "the Son can do nothing by himself; he can only do what he sees his Father doing, because whatever the Father does, the Son also does. For the Father loves the Son, and shows him all he does" (John 5:17–20). What an incredible challenge this is to all of us with the desire to change the world and address the injustices that we see.

Moses' reaction to this direct call is also instructive and not what one would expect from someone who once aspired to leadership. Moses, his self-confidence long ago shattered and further diminished by forty years of herding sheep far from any circle of political influence, professes himself to be incapable of doing what Jehovah demands and pleads with Him to "send someone else" (Exodus 4:1–17).

With respect to this concept of a direct calling to political action, I must confess to personally having no clear sense of a direct calling to enter federal politics or to found a new political party, though I employed the usual Christian tools for attempting to discern God's will on these matters: prayer, searching the Scriptures for guidance, and consulting fellow believers. And without in any way suggesting that my own experience is exemplary or denying that there is such a thing as a direct calling, my inclination is again to advise caution—caution demanding spiritual discernment—if one thinks that one has received such a direct calling to political action.

My inclination to advise caution comes from my experience of those who profess to having received such a calling more often than not being deceived. They have read into the call of God what is really the call of personal political ambition, the call of one's friends and supporters, or the call of political opportunity or necessity. For example, I knew an Alberta politician (Alberta is Canada's leading producer of oil and natural gas) who was sure he had seen a "burning bush" when in fact it turned out to be a gas flare. Again, this should raise questions for us. Does God, for instance, directly call believers to spiritually motivated political action today? And, how can one distinguish between a divine calling and other callings?

The Call to Be as Distinct from the Call to Do

There is much more to the story of Scripture, however, than just the call to do. Since leaving the active political arena and having more time to reflect on these matters than when in the heat of battle, I have been led to give much more weight to another kind of calling. It is the call to *be* as distinct from the call to *do*—the call to be a person motivated and shaped by the person of Jesus and to an intimate relationship with Him. It is out of this deeper call that the call to do will eventually flow.

The call to be is embedded throughout the biblical story. I find it particularly significant that the Apostle Peter (a man of action if there ever was one), in the light of cataclysmic predictions concerning the destruction of the current world order, did not give early believers a to-do list. Rather he said, "Since all these things are going to happen [my paraphrase], what kind of people ought you to *be*? You ought to live holy and godly lives as you look forward to the day of God and speed its coming" (2 Peter 3:11). The same call is made to us today, in spite of whatever cataclysmic predictions might be made around us.

In conclusion, I believe that there is such a thing as God's *call to do*—including the call to political service like Moses at the burning bush. That said, I think such callings are relatively rare and require great discernment to distinguish the true from the false. Even more importantly, however, there is the *call to be*—the call to be the kind of people God wants us to be. This is the higher calling out of which the call to action in partnership with God will flow. This all leads me to the concluding question upon which I urge reflection and application to our own lives: Have we heard and responded to the call to be?

Faith and Politics in the Life of Moses

This is a call most clearly described by the Apostle Paul in his letter to the Ephesians, and with which I will conclude this article:

> I urge you to live a life worthy of *the calling you have received.* Be completely humble, be gentle, be patient, bearing with one another in love . . . *Be no longer infants*, tossed back and forth by the waves, and blown here and there by every wind of teaching . . . Instead *(be truthful)*, speaking the truth in love. Put off the old self . . . and *be made new* in the attitude of your minds . . . Put on the new self . . . *be like God* in true righteousness. *Be kind and compassionate* to one another, forgiving each other, just as in Christ God forgave you . . . *Be imitators of God*, as dearly loved children, and live a life of love, just as Christ loved us and gave himself up for us . . . *Be very careful* then how you live . . . *Be wise* not unwise, making the most of every opportunity . . . *Be not foolish* but understanding what the will of the Lord is . . . Be filled with the Spirit . . . *Be thankful* to God the Father for everything in the name of our Lord Jesus Christ. (Ephesians 4:1–3, 14, 23–24, 32; 5:1–2, 15, 17–18, 20; emphasis added)

Notes

1. Note that it was the failure to wait which would later doom the leadership of Saul, Israel's first king, to both spiritual and political failure (1 Samuel 13:1–15).

2

At Work with God

Having explored the call to the political arena in the first chapter, this second chapter looks at the work of political action. While politics is a public arena for discourse and debate, it is ultimately an arena for action. It is an arena for mobilizing public opinion, contesting elections, representing and serving constituents, making policy, legislating, and governing. For those involved in politics, these are the actions that will be undertaken—and will be shaped by our Christian faith. By focusing again on the life of Moses, we will see the fundamental relationship between God's character, his active presence in the world, and our own actions in the political world. Ultimately, it is God's self-revelation that should shape our life and political action.

God Reveals Himself to Moses

Before looking at Moses' political action, it is important

to understand how God revealed himself, and the way he was at work, to Moses throughout his life. There are four distinct revelations that I have identified and will reflect on throughout this article:

1. God reveals himself as the eternally present *I Am* to Moses personally at the burning bush (Exodus 3). This is the *liberator* God who has come to free his captive people from bondage in Egypt in a political act.
2. God reveals himself as *warrior*—the God who fights for his people—at the Red Sea where the Egyptian army and cavalry are miraculously destroyed (Exodus 14). In ecstasy Moses pens a victory song rejoicing that "The Lord has hurled the horse and its rider into the sea" (Exodus 15).
3. God reveals himself as *lawmaker* and *judge* at Mount Sinai where Moses receives the Ten Commandments (Exodus 19, 20).
4. God reveals himself again at Mount Sinai as the God of *love, mercy, grace,* and *compassion* when Moses is summoned a second time to the top of the mountain (Exodus 34). God is not only just but also the God who forgives sin—even the sin of rebellion.

Moses' response to each of these revelations of God's character and activity profoundly shaped his spiritual and political leadership. Just as they were instructive for Moses, they are also instructive for any believer today seeking to relate his or her faith to political involvement.

The Need for God's Revelation

Once Moses had fresh insights into God as the liberator of Israel, and God as lawgiver and judge, he was able to join in the work he perceived God to be doing. While this participation was somewhat reluctant in the case of returning to Egypt—where his previous self-directed liberation effort had failed (as we explored in the first article)—it was wholehearted when it came to proclaiming and administering the Law of God to Israel.[1]

It is helpful to reflect on our own experience of receiving and acting upon a fresh understanding of who God is and what he is doing. Have you ever received a fresh understanding of who God is and/or seen him at work politically? Did you see it as a call to join in that work? Seeing where God is already at work can help us to clearly discern the difference between the call to political action that is rooted in faith and the call to political action that is otherwise motivated and self-directed.

With respect to my own experience with Christians

in Canadian politics, I would venture to say that most of us, regrettably, have *not* had any fresh understanding of God's character or activity in our country which can truly inspire or direct our personal political efforts. In western Canada we do have examples from our past like church ministers J.S. Wordsworth and Tommy Douglas (on the left) and Christian laymen like William Aberhart and my father Ernest C. Manning (on the right), all of whom were specifically inspired by their Christian convictions to found political movements that would address the suffering and injustices of the Great Depression. But despite these examples, our current generation of Christian-oriented political activists is more like Moses in Egypt *before* his burning-bush experience. We are engaged in well-intended efforts to address the political challenges of the day but—rather than stemming from a revelation of God—these efforts are largely self-directed.

We see injustices—income inequality or the intergenerational injustice of chronic deficit spending, for example—and are moved to do something political to address them. But I question whether such efforts are really any different from those efforts whose motivations and approaches to the same injustices are rooted in humanism, the social sciences, and secular political philosophies. If this assessment is correct and they are no different, then it points to our desperate need for a fresh revelation of God's character and work in our time. If we are to bring anything more than human resources to bear on addressing the ills of society, we need a revelation such as Moses had—a revelation of God as liberator, for instance.

Rather than look for a fresh revelation of God, we often rely on whatever has become our favourite conception of God and how he operates. In my opinion, the revelation of God as warrior became Moses' favourite conception. This may have been because military command was part of Moses' upbringing in Pharaoh's household.[2] Or perhaps it was because Moses anticipated the future military battles that Israel would face in order to occupy the Promised Land. As a political and religious leader, Moses found his greatest security in God as the one who fights for his people.

This aspect of Moses' experience raises the following questions for us as Christians: Do we have a favourite conception of Jesus that particularly influences our Christian calling and activity? Is there an aspect of Jesus' character or work that especially draws us to him? You might be particularly attracted to Jesus the teacher, Jesus the healer, Jesus the friend of the poor, or Jesus in some other role. For Moses, however, there was no one revelation that would see him through all of what he was called to do. Likewise, there might be revelations of God which challenge or expand those favourite conceptions to which we cling.

The Motivation for Political Action

For those who are politically inclined, it may well be that our favourite picture is of Jesus as the political activist. This is a picture that is often defined by the image of Jesus driving the money changers out of the temple (John 2:13–17)—a public and political act which his politically ambitious disciples greatly admired and longed to imitate. Not surprisingly, this incident brought to their minds a relevant quotation from the Psalms of David: "Zeal for [God's] house consumes me" (Psalm 69:9). Certainly this conception of Jesus has been attractive for Christians through the ages, from the Crusaders to members of the Moral Majority. But is this conception of Jesus the political activist one from which politically inclined Christians today should take their lead?

In my case (as a politician who favours "bottom up" democratic processes), it is Jesus' interaction with the public that I find most attractive. We see it as he travelled from town to town communicating his unique message, speaking persuasively to small groups of common people—occasionally making major addresses in the synagogues or to larger groups—and, of course, public jousting with his opponents. Anyone who has tried to build a grassroots political movement or engaged in a political campaign to convince large numbers of people to support a cause cannot help but admire the genius and achievements of Jesus in this regard.

But what about political action rooted in religious zeal? Importantly, while Jesus was motivated to purify his Father's house by religious zeal, he was able to exercise self-control over this zeal. His disciples, however, had much to learn before they could do likewise. For example, their uncontrolled zeal to advance the Kingdom would one day lead them to propose burning down a Samaritan village because it had rejected their master (Luke 9:51–55). Jesus had to rebuke them and expressly forbid them to have anything to do with the Samaritans (Matt.10:5) until they were fully imbued with his Spirit (Acts 1:8; 8:4–17).

In my experience, there is great danger when uncontrolled religious zeal is translated into political action. This danger needs to be scrupulously guarded against. Most significantly, the antidote to destructive religious zeal is to be found in the very same Psalm of David of which the disciples had remembered only a part. David himself knew what it meant to be consumed by religious zeal for political ends. But he was also well aware that when such zeal is not controlled by God's Spirit it can lead to actions which disgrace the people of God and repel those who might otherwise seek him. Hence David begins that same Psalm by first praying: "May those who hope in you not be disgraced because of me. . . . May those who seek you not be put to shame because of me" (Psalm 69:6).

There is definitely inspiration and guidance for the politically motivated Christian in the example and teachings of Jesus the public man. But lest we become dangerously consumed by zeal for the cause let us, like David, pray: "May nothing I do or say out of zeal for the work of Christ cause the Christian community to be disgraced or those who might seek him to be repelled because of me."

Responding to God as Grace

Finally, we come to Moses fourth and last great revelation of God's character and his *modus operandi* in the world. It came when Moses and the people of Israel had been ordered to leave Mount Sinai and proceed to the Promised Land. God offered to send an angel before them but declared, "I will not go with you because you are a stiff necked people" (Exodus 33:3).

In one of his most revealing discourses, Moses responds by pleading with God not to send Israel forth unless God's presence accompanies them. God relents and replies, "My presence will go with you, and I will give you rest" (Exodus 33:15). But Moses wants more, looking specifically for assurance that God will manifest himself again as the warrior who fights for his people, pleading, "Now show me your glory" (Exodus 33:18). God responds by saying that, yes, he will manifest his glory, but through his chosen way—a different, yet greater, way to that which Moses asked for—and so responds, "I will show you my goodness (grace) ... mercy ... and compassion" (Exodus 33:19).

God orders Moses to once again ascend Mount Sinai with two more tablets of stone on which the Law will be re-inscribed (Exodus 34:1–3). When he obeys God Moses receives this incomparable revelation of the character and work of God:

Then the Lord came down in the cloud and stood there with him and proclaimed his name, the Lord. And he passed in front of Moses, proclaiming, "The Lord, the Lord, the compassionate and gracious God, slow to anger, abounding in love and faithfulness, maintaining love to thousands, and forgiving wickedness, rebellion and sin. Yet he does not leave the guilty unpunished; he punishes the children and their children for the sin of the fathers to the third and fourth generation" (Exodus 43:5–7).

Sadly, this is the revelation of God which Moses seemed to have the greatest difficulty comprehending and accepting. Perhaps it was the assertion that God is even prepared to forgive rebellion—something Moses could never quite bring himself to do. While Moses never tired of reminding Israel of God the liberator, God the warrior, and God the lawgiver, what he heard and saw when he ascended Mount Sinai a second time is scarcely mentioned in his final addresses to Israel.

How, then, might we embrace this fourth revelation of the nature of God and his work in the world, and let it be instructive to us today?

Think back to your favourite conception of Jesus. It might be that of Jesus as the political activist. It might be Jesus as the one full of zeal. Or it might be Jesus as the man of the people. While there is value to each of these conceptions, for me, politics at the highest level is ultimately about the reconciliation of conflicting interests. If that is the case, then shouldn't the revelation of Jesus that most motivates and guides us be that of Jesus as the Saviour and reconciler of human beings to God and to each other? Surely it is this conception of Jesus—Jesus as the ultimate manifestation of God's grace, mercy, compassion, and forgiveness—that we should most faithfully and vigorously seek to represent in our personal relationships, in the marketplace, and in the public square.

Notes

1. As Moses' experience shows, some revelations of God will be more appealing to us than others.

2. According to Josephus, Moses himself once led an Egyptian military force into Ethiopia (*Antiquities of the Jews*, 2.9.2–2.11.1).

3

The Rule of Law

In the previous chapter, we explored how God invites his people to join with him in work by giving them a fresh revelation of his character. We saw this principle in operation as Moses' life was impacted through four distinct revelations of the character and work of God. In this article we return to the third of these revelations he received: God as *lawmaker* and *judge*.

Throughout Moses' life, it was this aspect of God that he most consistently represented to the people of Israel, so much so that in later years the Law of God came to be referred to as the Law of Moses (cf. Joshua 8:32; 2 Kings 23:25; John 7:23). What, then, were the implications for Moses and the children of Israel of seeing God as lawmaker and judge? And what might be the implications for us today? As we shall see, the lessons learned from this revelation and its aftermath are instructive for anyone involved in the formation or enforcement of rules.

The Rule of Law

The revelation of God as lawmaker and judge is most clearly seen in Moses' receiving of the Ten Commandments on Mount Sinai (Exodus 19–20). These commandments became part of a body of divinely inspired laws that Moses would communicate to the Israelites—laws intended to govern their relationship both with God and with each other. In its totality this body of law covered every aspect of the Israelites' personal, family, and national life, and was accompanied by promises of great blessings for obedience and threats of dire consequences for disobedience (cf. Deuteronomy 27–30). The aftermath of this revelation is recorded in the Old Testament as a 400-year-long endeavour to establish right relationships through law.

In my opinion, this record constitutes one of the most thorough and original textbooks in all of sacred and secular literature on what can and cannot be achieved through the rule of law. As such, there are lessons that rule-makers and rule-enforcers of every kind can learn from studying this record, no matter where they find themselves in the community. These lessons are especially relevant to legislators, however, as the making of law is one of the chief tasks of those elected to our federal parliament, provincial and territorial legislatures, and municipal councils.

The Benefits of Law

One of the lessons to be gleaned from studying law in the biblical record is that whenever and wherever laws are just—and justly administered—the benefits to individuals and society are many and abundant. These benefits—seen throughout history—include the constraint of evil, the protection of human rights, order throughout civil society, and the direction of resources toward beneficial ends. In Canada, the Rule of Law is recognized in our constitution as one of the fundamental principles on which the country itself is founded, and is essential to the achievement of "peace, order, and good government".

The benefits achievable through right law align with Scripture's constant emphasis that adherence to the Law of God is both a means of doing God's will and of receiving his blessing. I see this emphasized in Deuteronomy, as Moses commands the Israelites "to love the Lord your God . . . and to keep his commands, decrees, and laws" because by doing so they "will live and increase, and the Lord your God will bless you" (Deut. 30:16). The same emphasis can be seen in the Psalms as David declares blessed those "who walk according to the law of the Lord" and "who keep his statutes and seek him with all their heart" (Psalm 119:1–2). And, of course, it is emphasized by Jesus himself in his preface to the Sermon on the

Mount: "Think not that I have come to abolish the Law and the Prophets; I have not come to abolish them, but to fulfill them. I tell you the truth, until heaven and earth disappear, not the smallest letter, not the least stroke of the pen, will by any means disappear from the Law until everything is accomplished" (Matt. 5:17–18).

Jesus, David, and Moses all understood the importance of law and the blessing that it can confer upon those who follow it. Jesus in particular also understood the limits to law and the manner in which it can be abused.

The Abuse of Law

Evil cannot abolish an instrumentality—such as the rule of law—which has been established by God and intended for good. Lacking the ability to do away with the rule of law, the age-old tactic of the evil one is to pervert it toward evil ends. This perversion can take a number of forms. For example, while one of the possible benefits of law is freedom, one of the most effective ways of suppressing a freedom is to smother it via excessive rule-making and regulation. Consider, as an illustration of this perversion, the comprehensive state regulation of religious freedom in the former Soviet Union and present day China.

Throughout the ministry of Jesus, he frequently addressed the abuse of law and the spirit-quenching effects of excessive legalism. For example, he vehemently denounced the practice of making law a burden rather than a blessing, rebuking the Pharisees—the custodians of Moses' law—for laying "heavy burdens" on the people's shoulders and not lifting a finger to relieve them (Matthew 23).

Jesus likewise condemned the abuse of law through inconsistent and hypocritical practice: "Woe unto you, teachers of the law and Pharisees, you hypocrites! You give a tenth of your spices—mint, dill, and cumin [i.e. you keep the law in small matters]. But you have neglected the more important matters of the law—justice, mercy, and faithfulness. You should have practiced the latter, without neglecting the former" (Matthew 23:23).

The worst abuses of the rule of law, however, are those where laws are deliberately harnessed to the practice of evil. Jesus himself, for example, was the recipient of one of the most twisted abuses of law imaginable. In the lead up to his crucifixion, Jesus is brought by the chief priests and Pharisees to stand trial before the Roman governor, Pilate. But Pilate is unable to find Jesus guilty of violating any Roman law and is prepared to let him go. His legalistic accusers, however, declare that Jesus is a blasphemer and that, according to Moses' law, "he has to die because he has made himself the Son of God" (John 19:7). The

Law of God is twisted to such a degree that it is used to kill the Son of God.

Thus the rule of law—even the rule of the Law of God—is a two-edged sword. It is capable of being harnessed to achieve enormous benefits, but is also capable of doing enormous harm when abused. To protect the rule of law from being discredited, those who value and practise it must scrupulously guard against its abuse.

The Limits to Law

While we see the benefits and abuses of law in Scripture, I think the greatest lesson we can learn from Israel's experience with the rule of law concerns the limitations of law and lawmaking. This is another lesson relevant to all rule-makers and enforcers, whether they are parents in the home, leaders in the church, managers in the workplace, or law-makers in the political arena.

As discussed above, the Law of God was conceived and promulgated in order to establish and maintain right relationship between Israel and God, as well as among the Israelites themselves. The latter day prophets, however, came reluctantly to a sobering conclusion regarding the success of this attempt to achieve right relations by means of law alone. They concluded that laws—even those coming directly from the hand of God—are insufficient in themselves to achieve righteousness and justice. According to the prophets, unless law is accompanied by an internal transformation—inscribed on human hearts, not merely on tablets of stone—it is insufficient to achieve righteousness, justice, and good behaviour (cf. Jeremiah 31:31–33; Ezekiel 11:19–20; cf. 2 Corinthians 3:3).

It was, in part, the prophets' realization of the limitations of the rule of law that led them to long so fervently for the Messiah's coming. They longed for the one whose coming Moses prophesied because he would fulfil the mission of the law by becoming the means for the inner transformation required to obey it (Deuteronomy 18:15).

Implications for Us

What then can we learn from the experience of Moses and the Israelites with respect to the rule of law—its benefits, abuses, and limits—whether we are a rule maker in a home, church, or other organization; or in a legislature; or simply as a citizen and member of a community?

To enjoy the benefits of law, I think it is essential that Christians first recognize their responsibilities as citizens to work—whenever and wherever possible—within the strictures of the rule of law; we should be law-abiding citizens who follow the rule of law. That does not mean, however, that we should pay blind allegiance to those laws we consider unjust or ill-advised. But we should do our utmost to change rather than violate those laws—working with, rather than against, the rule of law.

There are also lessons we can learn from the outworking of the rule of law in Israel as we respond to it within our own Christian communities. Primarily, there is a need to acknowledge and deal with the ways in which we abuse the law and disrespect its limits. Rather than relying on grace and looking towards inner transformation, we far too often attempt to achieve right behaviour through rules often of our own making—multiplying and strictly enforcing them, despite our creedal acknowledgement of the all-sufficiency of the grace of God.

Rules, of course, have their necessary place in guiding us through the establishment of wise boundaries. But how many young people have been turned away from the faith of their parents by too much law and not enough grace? Rules of worship and conduct are necessary to shape, guide, and protect a spiritual community—hence the law given to Moses for the benefit of Israel, and rules of worship and conduct for Christians today. But many seekers and believers today refuse to darken a church door because all they have ever encountered there was a dry and pharisaical Christian legalism. Recognizing the limitations of the law is a step towards creating a grace-filled space in which people can return to God.

Outside of our own Christian community, what might be the implications of these "lessons from Moses" for society-at-large? In particular, to what extent have our parliaments, legislatures, and municipal councils—as lawmaking bodies—come to grips with the limitations of law?

As stated above, law may be beneficially used to accomplish many worthwhile objectives—including the constraint of evil, the protection of human rights, order throughout civil society, and the direction of resources toward beneficial ends. But when legislators seek to use law to reach far beyond such objectives—when we declare or imply that we can create a "just society," a Canada "strong and free," or a true north utopia simply by enacting legislation and implementing public policies, we deceive ourselves and our constituents by ignoring the limitations of law.

In theory, of course, our legislatures could pass laws requiring each of us to love our neighbour as ourselves and requiring public servants to love their clients as themselves. But the implication of the Israelite story is that such laws would be of little effect and insufficient in themselves to achieve such ends. As the Apostle Paul declares in his letter to the Galatians, if a law could have been framed which imparted "life" in all its abundance to

Israel and mankind, then righteousness and justice would have come by the Law of Moses (Galatians 3:21). If the Law of God was so severely limited in its ability to produce such results, why should we believe that our own laws could do so? In fact, having seen the way law can be abused, we should be warned that it is precisely those laws which reach for utopia that can most easily be turned into instruments of oppression. Such is what comes from failing to recognize the limitations of law and seeking to achieve ends beyond those limits.

Should this frank and honest acknowledgement of the limits of law lead to disillusionment and the abandonment of hope for a better country? Or is there a source of hope that we can hold onto? As the Apostle Paul so clearly pointed out, the realization of the law's limits shouldn't lead us to despair, but instead to search for righteousness and justice in another source (Galatians 3:23–25). While Moses only dimly perceived that source, it is fully revealed to us in the New Testament as Jesus—the fulfiller of the law through the transformation of hearts. And it is in him that our hope lies. "For the law came by Moses but grace and truth came by Jesus Christ" (John 1:17).

4

The Role of the Leader

As we have seen throughout this study, there are many lessons that we can learn from the life of Moses. In this chapter, we will look to learn from Moses' role as both a spiritual and political leader, and try to understand what the role of the leader is fundamentally about. Although the initial call Moses received was to lead the Israelites out of Egypt, that task was only the start of his leadership. Through the journey in the wilderness, Moses' role shifted from being an inspirational, revolutionary leader to leading a reluctant people on a depressing detour of their own making, away from and not toward the better future originally envisioned for them. As we will see in this article, Moses was instrumental in acting as a mediator between God and the people; in the institutionalization of values and practices; and, finally, in serving the people by preparing for a successor to lead in his inevitable absence. At the heart of all that Moses did was the recognition that his leadership was not about self-glorification. Instead, it was about serving one greater than himself and joining in his work.

Leadership as Mediation

To understand the role of the leader, it is important to first establish what lies at the heart of leadership. Through my experience in politics, I've come to see that leadership of any kind and at any level invariably involves the reconciliation of conflicting interests. In Moses' case this meant not only mediating disputes among the Israelites themselves, but also acting as a mediator between God and his people.

Initially, of course, Moses acted as a mediator between God, the Israelites, and Pharaoh. But once the Red Sea had been crossed, Moses began to face intense criticism from the people he was leading (a topic we will explore more deeply in the next article). Despite being freed from slavery, they resented the hardships of the desert journey toward the Promised Land and frequently demanded a return to Egypt. Most often their criticisms were directed at Moses as God's representative, forcing Moses to stand in the gap between God and his people.

For example, when the Israelites (after receiving the negative report from the spies) refused to enter the Promised Land, God threatened to destroy them and start all over again by creating a new nation from Moses' own descendants. But Moses interceded as a mediator on their behalf, reciting back to God the promise he had declared to Moses on Mount Sinai: "The Lord is slow to anger, abounding in love and forgiving sin and rebellion" (Numbers 14:11–19).

But perhaps the most striking example of Moses as mediator occurred when venomous snakes were sent among the people in response to yet another outbreak of rebellion. Again Moses interceded in prayer for the people, and God responded by instructing him to make a bronze snake and put it up on a pole. Whoever looked at the bronze snake, after being bitten, would live (Numbers 21:4–9). In the New Testament, Jesus specifically refers to this incident as analogous to his own role as a sin bearer and his mediatory death on the cross—"Just as Moses lifted up the snake in the desert, so the Son of Man must be lifted up, that everyone who believes in him may have eternal life" (John 3:14).

As Christians, no matter what position we occupy in society or in an organization, we are called to practise the ministry of reconciliation. In doing so we are acting out one of the most central doctrines of our faith (2 Corinthians 5:17–21). And while this is not the place to expand on all that the ministry of reconciliation involves, it is nevertheless instructive to recognize that mediation was one of the central tasks of Moses the political and spiritual leader, and that in this regard he models leadership in the spirit of Christ.

Institutionalising for the Future

While dealing with issues at hand through mediation is an unavoidable aspect of leadership, it is also critical to prepare for the future if the values, mission, and distinctive character of the organization or community is to be sustained over the long run. Such preparation includes more than succession planning; in particular it includes institutionalising those values and practices necessary to achieve long run sustainability.

Thus—on instruction from God—Moses communicated to the children of Israel the legal, material, and procedural/ceremonial means whereby they were to worship and serve Him and one another. In fact, more than sixty chapters of the Pentateuch are devoted to descriptions and instructions pertaining to how the Israelites were meant to live with respect to their treatment of one another and resolving conflicts; how they were to celebrate the Sabbath and various feasts and festivals; how they were to worship individually and communally, and the role of priests within worship; what they were to eat, and the means by which they were to stay healthy; and the various punishments and blessings for their responses to these instructions.

On the surface these laws may look like mere religious trappings. On closer inspection, however, they were about preparing the community for the future. In fact, all these regulations are means to facilitate the end of bringing glory to God through worship, obedience, and service. In order for the future to be prepared for, the correct end had to be kept as the central concern.

But as the historian Will Durant has ruefully observed, "It is the tragedy of things spiritual, that they languish if unorganized and yet are corrupted by the material [and, I would add, intellectual] means of their organization." True to Durant's observation, many of the laws, structures, and ceremonies established under Moses and meant to facilitate the worship and service of God became, by Jesus' time, ends in themselves. Moses' Law had become corrupted to such a degree that, in Jesus' judgment, the Temple was now a "den of thieves"; the Sabbath a wearisome burden; and the law itself was more about splitting hairs than about justice and mercy. The Rule of Law established by Moses had tragically degenerated for the most part into a dry and spiritually bankrupt legalism. It was perverted to the point where the Pharisees could even say to Pilate "we have a law [the Law of God], and by our law he [the Son of God] ought to die" (John 19:7).

Any worthwhile pursuit—spiritual, political, economic, academic, or charitable—needs to be organized in some fashion if it's to be sustained. More often than not, this is the leader's responsibility. When done well, institutionalising sustains the life and purpose of the enterprise. But far too often the means of institutionalising can quench the spirit of an organisation. It takes wise leadership indeed to discern what leads to life and what leads to death. Being acutely aware of these possibilities, however, is the first step toward preventing institutionalisation from eventually strangling the organization or community it is meant to sustain.

Preparing for Succession

Providing for a qualified successor is often one of the last and most trying tasks of leadership. This task is complicated by the fact that there will be many others with distinct ideas as to who your successor should be.

During Moses' long tenure as Israel's political and spiritual leader there were several attempts to displace or replace him as leader—by members of his own household (Numbers 12:1–16); by angry mobs of discontented and disillusioned followers (Numbers 14:1–4, 10); and even by the community leaders he had appointed (Numbers 16).

But instead, God had Joshua in mind as a successor for Moses. And perhaps Moses was vaguely aware of this from an early stage as he assigned Joshua to lead the Israelites in one of their earliest battles (Exodus 17:10). He also picked Joshua to serve as his aide at the Tent of Meeting where Moses met face to face with God (Exodus 33:7–11). Likewise, Joshua was selected as one of the twelve spies to explore Canaan, and on the completion of this mission only he and Caleb still believed that God could give the Israelites the land (Numbers 13:8; 14:5–9). It seems like Joshua was being prepared by God, long before he ever received the mantle of leadership from Moses.

Eventually Moses was clearly directed to "commission Joshua, and encourage and strengthen him, for he will lead this people across [the Jordan] and will cause them to inherit the land" (Deuteronomy 3:28). By largely leaving succession and his own reputation in the hands of God, Moses left the leadership of Israel in capable hands as Joshua went on to fulfill the mission of leading the children of Israel into the Promised Land.

The Leader's Legacy

At the end of the day, perhaps the greatest lesson we can

learn from Moses is that true leadership isn't about the leader. It's about serving someone and something greater than one's self.

One of the most admirable things about Moses is that, unlike many modern leaders, he was not preoccupied in his latter years with creating a personal legacy. My father, who spent all of his adult years in politics and government, twenty-five as Premier of Alberta, described the dangers of a leader trying too hard to shape his own legacy while still in office: "It's like trying to drive a car forward while looking in the rear view mirror. The most likely result will be a crash—and that will be your legacy."

Moses for the most part was willing to leave not only the choice of his successor but also his legacy in the hands of God. He made no provision for members of his family, or even members of his own tribe, to succeed him. He erected no monument to himself, named no institution after himself, and even his gravesite is known only to God. He steadfastly served his people by serving the one who had called him to that service and to whom he was ultimately accountable. And what a legacy of leadership that left for Israel and for us. The Books of Moses conclude with this fitting epitaph to Israel's first political and spiritual leader: "No prophet has risen in Israel like Moses whom the Lord knew face to face" (Deuteronomy 34:10).

5

The Challenges of Leadership

In the previous chapter we looked at the *role* of the leader. In this chapter we will focus on the *challenges* a leader invariably faces in the course of living out that role. From examining some of the specific challenges Moses faced as a political leader, we will see that many of these are similar to those faced by people in positions of leadership today. They include the burden of overwork and the need to delegate; the constant encroachment of work and leadership obligations on personal and family life; and coping with a steady stream of complaints, opposition, and threats to the leader's position.

As we face these challenges we must remember that Moses was not just a political leader. He was first and foremost a spiritual leader—a man of faith to whom God had graciously revealed himself and his work. So what difference did this make in how he handled the challenges of leadership? And what lessons are there for us, as we take the necessary step of relating *our* faith to *our* calling, work, and leadership obligations?

The Wisdom and Risks of Delegation

The first challenge that Moses faced—like many leaders past and present—was overwork. There is always more to do than there are hours in the day. So Moses learns the wisdom of delegation. Shortly after leading the Israelites out of Egypt, Moses was visited by his father-in-law Jethro. Having observed that Moses was overworked, Jethro urged him to delegate some of his responsibilities to "officials over thousands, hundreds, fifties, and tens." Moses followed this wise advice (Exodus 18) with the apparent approval of God (Exodus 18:23) and the people (Deuteronomy 1:9–18).

Throughout his time as a leader, Moses was directed by God to further distribute the responsibilities of spiritual and temporal leadership. Notably, he established the Aaronic priesthood and the Levitical order to care for the tabernacle—an important aspect of spiritual leadership for the Israelites. He also anointed seventy elders of Israel with God's Spirit "to carry the burden of the people so he would not have to carry it alone" (Numbers 11:10–17). One further example of Moses's delegation is how—in response to the Lord's direction and his own inclination—Moses gave the job of scouting out the Promised Land to a task force of twelve men—one being chosen from each tribe (Numbers 13:1).

Many leaders, however, are reluctant to delegate and unwilling to relinquish their power despite this being a means by which they can better serve the community they are leading. This reluctance might be due to egocentricity, personal insecurities, or a lack of faith in the abilities and motives of others—three often inter-related character flaws. While Moses had his own set of insecurities, they do not seem to have found expression in a reluctance to delegate.

Sadly, though, Moses's delegation did not always lead to positive outcomes for himself or the people. The most obvious disappointment was the betrayal of purpose by the task-force Moses appointed to scout the Promised Land. This was a betrayal which led to the drastic result of Israel's having to wander in the wilderness for forty years. Similarly, the community leaders to whom Moses had delegated responsibility were also those who—at the instigation of Korah, Dathan, and Abiram—later led the rebellion against his leadership and God's direction (Numbers 16). While it is often wise to delegate, there are obvious risks in doing so and the outcomes of that delegated leadership cannot be guaranteed.

My own experience with delegation has included a reluctance to delegate, because as a perfectionist "I'd rather do it myself and get it right" than delegate the wrong task to the wrong party and then be forced to devote endless amounts of time trying to correct the mis-delegation. My observation is that when we view our co-workers as simply "functional beings" we tend to attach too much weight to whether they possess the functional capacity and experience required to accomplish the task, and we pay insufficient attention to whether or not they have a heart prepared for and attuned to the job.

When we view our co-workers and colleagues from a more spiritual perspective—as "human beings" and therefore suffering from the consequences of the fall but also bearing in some way the image of God—we should be less inclined to lean solely on our own human wisdom in making delegation decisions, and be more apt to seek guidance from him who sees the hearts of all people.

Knowing when and what to delegate, and to whom, is an integral part of leadership to which are attached both benefits and risks. It is sobering to remember that even Moses, the man of God, was not immune to ill-advisedly placing trust in those to whom he delegated authority and responsibilities, and that we ourselves are not immune to misplacing our own trust when we delegate. All the more reason to seek spiritual insight and guidance in delegating responsibilities to others.

Protecting Family Life

Undoubtedly one of the biggest challenges any leader faces is adequately safeguarding personal and family relations against the relentless encroachment of leadership obligations. So let us consider this challenge in the case of Moses.

Having grown up in the courts of Egypt as a prince, Moses fled to Midian after killing an Egyptian. In Midian, Moses married Zipporah, a shepherdess daughter of a Midianite priest (Jethro). Zipporah bore Moses two sons, Gershom (Exodus 2:16–21) and Eliezer (Exodus 18:3–6). Together, Moses and Zipporah, along with their two sons, journeyed back to Egypt. One can only try to imagine the culture shock of a shepherdess from Midian going to Egypt on a mission to confront Pharaoh!

Apparently, at some point during the conflict with Pharaoh, Moses sent his wife and sons away—back to his father-in-law Jethro. When Jethro came to see Moses after the liberation of Israel from Egypt he brought Zipporah and their sons with him. What the Scripture records is Moses's enthusiastic reception of Jethro, but it says nothing at all about his reunion with Zipporah (Exodus 18:1–8).

Later in the story, Moses married a Cushite woman—much to the displeasure of Miriam and Aaron (Numbers 12:1)—and nothing more is said regarding Zipporah, Gershom, or Eliezer. Furthermore, although several of Aaron's sons were appointed to succeed him in the priesthood, Moses's sons are never mentioned as possible successors to his leadership.

Like many political and religious leaders, Moses' commitment to his leadership responsibilities appeared to damage his family relationships. The same tragedy occurred with Samuel and again with David, and "tragedy" is definitely the right word to describe this all-too-frequent phenomenon. In Canada, the incidence of family break up is higher among members of the House of Commons than it is among the general population.

My own experience in this area involves "trying to do both"—trying to satisfy the obligations to leadership and family equally and simultaneously. But this is an ill-advised course because in practice the immediate and incessant demands of leadership will inexorably take precedent over family obligations, leaving one's spouse with an unequal share of family responsibilities and inevitably depriving someone—a spouse, a child, a grandchild—of needed attention, affection, and guidance.

The God we serve is first and foremost a God who treasures relationships—our relationship with him and with each other. When we sacrifice these relationships, especially the relationship with family, to other pursuits—the pursuit of wealth, power, self-satisfaction and even such causes as public service or "doing God's work"—we are courting personal tragedy. God may call us to "self-sacrificial" service. But if that service involves involuntarily sacrificing the interests and well-being of others, especially members of our family, we need to earnestly seek his help in resolving the apparent contradiction.

It is important to ask, therefore, what safeguards are in place to insure that your leadership commitments—whatever spheres they may be in—do not adversely affect, or even destroy, your marriage or relations with your children. This is one area where, sadly, the example of Moses is not to be emulated.

Coping with Criticism, Opposition, and Threats

The greatest, most persistent, and most debilitating challenge of leadership that Moses experienced was coping with grumbling, complaining, criticism, opposition, and threats to his leadership from those he was attempting to lead. The Israelites grumbled about water at Marah (Exodus 15:22–25), and again at Rephidim (Exodus 17:1–7). And they complained about their lack of food in the Desert of Sin (Exodus 16), and again about their hardships at Taberah (Numbers 11).

On several occasions the criticism and complaining about Moses' leadership turned into outright rebellion—for example, when the Israelites received the negative report from the spies sent to scout out the promised land (Numbers 14:1–4, 10) and when Korah, Dathan, and Abiram challenged Moses' spiritual authority (Numbers 16). On the first of these occasions the people were even prepared to stone Moses and Aaron and replace them with leaders who would return them to Egypt—direct rebellion, not only against Moses and Aaron, but also against the will and purpose of God himself.

In the case of threats to his own leadership Moses did not defend himself but simply trusted in God to do so—leading to the description of Moses (a very unusual description of a revolutionary leader) as "a very humble man, more humble than anyone else on the face of the earth" (Numbers 12:3). And in each of the recorded cases of Israel grumbling and complaining to Moses about their lack of water or food, Moses took the criticism before the Lord and sought direction from him. In each of these cases, Moses followed God's direction and the people's needs were miraculously met.

One tragic incident at Kadesh, however, reveals a different response. Again the children of Israel were bitterly complaining to Moses and Aaron about the lack of water. Taking the people's petition before God, Moses was instructed to "tell the rock before their eyes to yield its water." Moses returned to the people, still bitter at their complaints, and said, "Listen, you rebels, must *we* [Moses and Aaron] bring you water out of this rock?" Then Moses, after seemingly attributing the forthcoming miracle to himself and Aaron rather than to God, struck the rock to bring forth water, instead of speaking to it as God had commanded. In failing to obey God's clear instructions, Moses and Aaron were severely censured:

And the Lord said to Moses and Aaron, "Because you did not believe in me, to uphold me as holy in the eyes of the people of Israel, therefore you shall not bring this assembly into the land that I have given them" (Numbers 20:12).

In sum, what can we learn from Moses's experience in dealing with the constant and intense criticism he received from the people he was called to lead, including direct threats to his leadership? Two things.

First, it is significant and admirable that Moses let

God deal with direct threats to his leadership rather than trying to defend himself. This required not only admirable restraint but also a deep faith and confidence that ultimately he owed his leadership position to divine providence and that ultimately it was in God's hands, not his or the people's, to sustain or revoke it. Might those of us in our leadership positions come to know such a deep faith and confidence in the sovereignty of God.

Second, without trying to dodge the question, perhaps another lesson from Moses' experience with criticism and internal opposition is not so much for the leader as it is for the followers. I can say from my own experience that constant criticism of a leader from within is more debilitating than all the attacks and criticisms from without. In Moses' case that criticism wore away at him and eventually resulted in his exasperated response at Kadesh. Consequently, it deeply and adversely affected his personal relationship with God and led directly to what he regarded as his greatest failure—his inability to take the people of God into the Promised Land.

Leaders—in particular political and spiritual leaders—are not beyond criticism, nor should they be. But when our grumbling, complaining, and criticism undermines not only their relationship with us but also their relationship with the ultimate source of their guidance and inspiration, then we have gone too far. We need lessons in leadership and there are plenty of those in the life of Moses. But there is also such a thing as godly and ungodly followership—and there are hard lessons to be learned on this front as well from the relationship between Moses and those he was called upon by God to lead.

6

Last Words

Special attention should always be paid to how leaders conclude their leadership and the words they use in doing so. It is usually in their last words to their friends and followers that the leader reveals what is weighing most heavily on their mind and heart as they look back over their career. And it is often in these last words that they emphasize what they consider most important to pass on to the next generation with a view to the future. What they leave unsaid is often equally significant. In this concluding chapter on faith and politics in the life of Moses let us therefore carefully examine his last addresses to the children of Israel as recorded in the Book of Deuteronomy.

Looking Back

In these addresses, Moses says little about the miraculous deliverance of the Israelites from Egypt, but instead begins to rehearse the Israelite story from when they received the Law of God at Mount Sinai. He recounts many significant events in the Israelites journey: their refusal to enter the Promised Land (Deuteronomy 1); their wanderings in the desert (Deuteronomy 2:1–15); their military victories (Deuteronomy 2:16–3:22); their experiences in receiving and learning to obey the Law (Deuteronomy 4–6); and the commissioning of Joshua as their next leader (Deuteronomy 31:1–8).

While Moses' most significant achievement was leading the liberation of Israel from slavery in Egypt, it is striking that he hardly mentions this accomplishment at all in these last addresses. Usually liberation movements and liberation leaders have the most to say on the theme of "freedom from"—identifying and rehearsing the evils and bondage from which they have delivered their followers. Often they have far less to say about "freedom to"—identifying and emphasizing the ends toward which the exercise of the newly gained freedom of their followers is to be directed.

This is not the case with Moses. He is very clear that Israel had been liberated *from* the bondage of Egypt *in order to* worship and serve the God who has delivered them. This is made explicit from the start of the exodus account where the Lord says to Pharaoh: "Let my son Israel go, so he may worship me" (Exodus 4:23). Thus Moses' last addresses to Israel focus heavily on urging them toward the goal of worshiping, obeying, and serving God.

This emphasis in Moses' final addresses is highly relevant to us as Christian believers. We are usually quite settled and articulate on the fact that God has delivered us from our sins. But sometimes we are less settled and articulate on the purposes to which this new found spiritual freedom is to be directed, such as living a Christ-like life. Like the Israelites, we need to be often and strongly reminded to exercise our "freedom to".

Looking Ahead

Moses also uses his last exhortations to turn the people's gaze towards the future by making several remarkable prophecies. Prominent among these is the promise of the coming Messiah: "The Lord your God will raise up for you a prophet like me from among your own brothers. You must listen to him" (Deuteronomy 18:15).

Moses also prophesies that once the Israelites are established in the land, they will desire to have a king "like all the nations around us" (Deuteronomy 17:14–20). Unlike Samuel, many years later (1 Samuel 8), Moses does not appear to oppose the idea of a monarchy. That said, he firmly insists that even the king is to be under the Law (a concept not fully established in Western democracy until the eighteenth century).

Furthermore, Moses prophesies Israel's future rebellion against God and the Law of God (Deuteronomy 31:14–22)—even composing a song on this theme (Deuteronomy 32). Perhaps because of his past experience and future forebodings with respect to Israel's predisposition to rebel against God the Lawgiver, Moses devotes much of his last addresses to Israel to reinforcing the rule of law (Deuteronomy 12–26). This reinforcement includes strong exhortations to love and obey the Lord and the law (Deuteronomy 11, 27:1–8; 29, 31:9–13); the pronouncement of dire curses for breaking or abandoning the law (Deuteronomy 27:9–26; 28:13–68); and the promise of great blessings and prosperity for adherence to the law (Deuteronomy 28:1–14; 30, 33). Through all these prophesies and warnings, Moses is directing the people toward the ultimate aim of their political and spiritual liberty—not freedom from the Egyptians, but freedom to worship God.

From Moses to Us

Looking back again over Moses' life, certain questions come to mind which further help establish the relevance of the "lessons from Moses" to our lives today. First, let us ask whether Moses fulfilled the "call to do." This was the call (examined in the first article of this series) to join with God in delivering the children of Israel from slavery in Egypt—the call he received at the burning bush. The answer to this is obviously yes. But what about each of us? How have we received and fulfilled our own "call to do"—to join with God in whatever he has shown himself to be doing in our time and circumstances? That is a question we must wrestle with and revisit throughout our lives.

As we saw, however, there is a more primary call that God makes to each of us: the "call to be." In Moses' case this was the call to be a leader submissive to the will of God. Again, I believe Moses answered this call—reluctantly at first but admirably in later years. The impetuous Egyptian prince, who once thought he could liberate Israel by himself, was transformed through spiritual and political experience into a man "more humble than anyone else on the face of the earth" (Numbers 12:2), and whose leadership had to be defended by God because he was reluctant to defend it himself (Number 12, 14, 16).

But again, what about us? Have we fulfilled the "call to be"—the call to be transformed by our spiritual and life experience into the likeness of Christ, who "humbled himself and became obedient unto death—even death on a cross" (Philippians 2:8). Again, wrestling with this question and being faithful in our responses to it should be a key aspect of our Christian walk.

There is a subsequent question which also comes to mind as we reflect on Moses' life: how did he receive his sense of mission? As we saw in the second article, Moses' sense of commission largely came through four distinct revelations of God and his work. The first of these was at the burning bush where God revealed himself as the eternally present *I Am* who would liberate his people. The second was at the Red Sea where God revealed himself as *warrior*. Later at Mount Sinai, God revealed himself first as *lawgiver* and *judge*, and then, when Moses ascended Sinai the second time, as the God of *grace*.

Again, what about us as Christians today? Have we ever received a fresh revelation of God and his work through Christ—a revelation which gives us a renewed sense of mission? Perhaps you have seen God anew as the creator and sustainer of life, inviting you to join him in creation care. Or possibly you have seen God anew as the one who constrains and overcomes evil, inviting us to take ethical stands at work or in the community? Or have seen God anew as the God of Grace who is reconciling all things (including ourselves) to himself and who invites us to join with him in the ministry of reconciliation? All of us need a revelation of God and his work if we are to be sustained and propelled as Christians into mission beyond our own limited capabilities.

Of course, paralleling Moses, each of us is likely to have a favourite conception of God. As such, we need to consider whether this is the most apt conception for us. In Moses' case, his favourite conception of God was not as grace but as warrior, which proved limiting for him. And so, what is our favourite conception of Jesus—Jesus as teacher? Jesus as healer? Jesus as political activist? Or Jesus as the reconciler of man to God through his self-sacrificial death on the cross? It is important to consider what dimensions of himself and his work God is revealing to us at particular times and in particular circumstances—in order to derive therefrom our own sense of mission.

One final question: what have we learned from the experience of Moses and the people of Israel concerning the Rule of Law—its benefits and its limits? If we value the Rule of Law, do we ourselves adhere to and support the law and the processes whereby our laws are made? And are we aware of the limits of rule-making—that utopia here on earth cannot be achieved by legislating, and that excessive rulemaking and enforcement can quench the spirit of our children and society?

The Strange Omission

In his last addresses to Israel, Moses recounts his second sojourn on Mount Sinai during which he received, for a second time, the tablets of the law (Deuteronomy 10:1–11). But, strangely and inexplicably from my perspective, Moses makes no mention in his last addresses of the revelation he received on that occasion of God as "grace, mercy, and compassion"—the one who demands justice but forgives sin, even the sin of rebellion.

Just prior to receiving that revelation, Moses had prayed for God to manifest his presence and glory, and God responded:

> The Lord came down in the cloud and stood there with him and proclaimed his name, the Lord. And he passed in front of Moses, proclaiming, "The Lord, the Lord, the compassionate and gracious God, slow to anger, abounding in love and faithfulness, maintaining love to thousands, and forgiving wickedness, rebellion (yes, rebellion), and sin. Yet he does not leave the guilty unpunished; he punishes the children and their children for the sin of the fathers to the third and fourth generation." (Exodus 34:5–7)

If you or I had received such a direct revelation of God as grace, would it not have been the highlight of our spiritual experience? Absolutely—and we would have wanted to share it with our contemporaries and to all of posterity! Yet Moses only mentioned this incident once in his writings, when he sought God's pardon for Israel's rebellious refusal to enter the Promised Land (Numbers 14:13–19). And, he never referred to it at all in his final addresses to Israel before his death.

As previously mentioned, it may have been that Moses never fully grasped the revelation of God as grace because it was overshadowed by his more favoured conception of God as warrior. Or perhaps it was that he had a great deal of difficulty believing that God could or should forgive rebellion, which was the sin he (understandably) had the most difficulty forgiving given the amount of grief it caused him during his career as a spiritual and political leader.

But before we are too hard on Moses, what about us? As Christians we have experienced the grace of Calvary, and so we too have received the great revelation of God as grace. As such, should that not be the highlight of our spiritual experience which we would most want to share with our own contemporaries? Or have we allowed valid but lesser revelations and experiences to overshadow "the great revelation"—God as grace as revealed in Christ?

Faith and Politics in the Life of Moses

Your Last Words

Having considered all of the above, if you had to give some last words to your family and friends, concerning your experience of God and his leading in your life, what would you emphasize?

If you had to give a final address to the Christian community or the public at large, concerning your experience of God's leading and the discharge of whatever leadership responsibilities you have been given, what would you include and exclude?

What might your last words to your workplace be, especially if it is a place where the spiritual is neither recognized nor honoured, but to which you may well have been called to serve as salt and light?

In my case, there came such a day on January 31, 2002. This was the day I spoke for the last time in the Canadian House of Commons—my place of work for nine lengthy years and reminiscent of the enormous amount of time and effort which my friends and I had expended to gain the seat I was now vacating.

The circumstances obliged me, of course, to extend well-deserved thanks to colleagues, staff, and constituents, and to reiterate my views on several of the major issues I had sought to advance. But I also wanted to end by emphasizing the spiritual in a chamber where reference to the spiritual was generally considered off limits. So I concluded by briefly referencing two subjects: the genetic revolution and the terrorist attacks of September 11, 2001. These were (and are) two subjects fraught with moral implications of the type which our Parliament is loathe to even recognize, let alone debate. And so, in concluding this series, my last words to Parliament are the words I want to leave you with:

> In days past, we . . . have avoided such debate like the plague. But while it is a mistake to see moral issues where they do not in fact exist, it is an even greater mistake to fail to see them when they actually arise.
>
> Responsible leadership in such circumstances will require parliamentarians to engage on such issues—openly, honestly, respectfully, and cautiously—but to engage nonetheless. . . . I wish you success as you venture forward on this frontier.
>
> And in the spirit of this necessity to engage more openly on matters of faith and morality, I leave you with my favourite prayer by a nineteenth-century statesman and democrat, who wrestled long and hard with such issues, and which he gave on the occasion of his departure from his political friends.
>
> "Trusting in Him, who can go with me and remain with you and be everywhere for good, let us

confidently hope that all will be well. . . . To His care commending you, as I hope in your prayers you will commend me, I bid you an affectionate farewell."[1]

Notes

1. Abraham Lincoln's farewell address, Springfield, Illinois, February 11, 1861.

Preston Manning served as a member of the Canadian House of Commons from 1993 to 2001. He founded two new political parties—the Reform Party of Canada and the Canadian Reform Conservative Alliance—and was the Leader of the Official Opposition from 1997 to 2000. In 2005, he founded the Manning Centre for Building Democracy, which supports research, educational, and communications initiatives designed to achieve a more democratic society in Canada guided by conservative principles. He was appointed a Companion of the Order of Canada in 2007 and has received honorary doctorates from five Canadian universities. Preston Manning became a Senior Fellow of the Marketplace Institute in January 2012.

CPSIA information can be obtained at www.ICGtesting.com
Printed in the USA
LVOW11s2113231013

358304LV00001B/1/P